SELF-PORTRAIT AS JERRY QUARRY

New Issues Poetry & Prose
The College of Arts and Sciences
Western Michigan University
Kalamazoo, MI 49008

An Inland Seas Poetry Book

Inland Seas poetry books are supported by a grant from
The Michigan Council for Arts and Cultural Affairs.

Printed in the United States of America.

First Edition, 2002.

ISBN 1-930974-19-1 (paperbound)

Library of Congress Cataloging-in-Publication Data:
Aiuto, Vito
Self-Portrait as Jerry Quarry/Vito Aiuto
Library of Congress Control Number: 2002104059

Art Direction	Joseph Wingard
Design	Cameron Pollard
Production	Paul Sizer
	The Design Center, Department of Art
	College of Fine Arts
	Western Michigan University

SELF-PORTRAIT AS JERRY QUARRY

VITO AIUTO

New Issues

WESTERN MICHIGAN UNIVERSITY

for my sister, Meggan January

Contents

One

Two

Three

Acknowledgments

These poems (or versions of them) appeared in the following publications:

Black Bear Review: "Consolation Prize," "Range (Blastocyst?)"

Black Creek Review: "Horse Stories" (1, 2, 3, and 4)

Crab Creek Review: "Temple, Temple"

De/Scribe: "Three Stories" (as "Three Poems")

Many Mountains Moving: "Three Pictures of My Wife" (as "Poem")

The Prairie Star: "Horse Stories" (13)

Poetry Motel: "Nothing in New York City"

RHINO 2001: "Revolutions Per Minute"

Theology Today: "For a Sick Friend"

"Friday Night" is in *The PrePress Awards, Volume II,* an anthology of emerging writers.

My gratitude to the following people for helping me with these poems by their counsel, encouragement, example and gracious listening: Monique Aiuto, Ruth Aiuto, Paula Bowman, Matt Cashen, Ruth Doan, Jay Ellis, Mike (Marshall) Faulkner, Andy Friedman, Melissa Herwaldt, John Rybicki, Sufjan Stevens, Scotty Utz.

And David Dodd Lee. And Jeremy Dowsett.

One

Of course we're not guilty
of what we've been accused of
but we're guilty of so much else, what's it matter . . .
—Dean Young

Consolation Prize

Although the word "assuage" is nicer
to look at than to say, that's what we're here
to do, assuage our guilt

among the ravaged paper flowers, the high-
school wrestling team drunk and high-fiving
on the veranda as they pass around
a certificate commending them for the size
of their long-distance telephone bill. The side

door screams metal on metal when anyone comes
or goes, but that's the way the staff likes it. As for me,

I think I'd rather be a little more
like the old guy who can't recollect my name
but who rushes to the threshold of weeping
every time he tells me about Israel's prophets:
Jonah diminishing in the whale's gut: tears well.
Jeremiah busting up the leaky cisterns: tears well.
Later, in the kitchen, he notices

I'm using the huge-ass toaster
as a mirror. I pretend to be fishing around in the fridge
for a broken and contrite heart,

but all I find is a plump link of sausage,
which I'm sure meant a broken heart
for some wretched head

of livestock locked
in an aluminum pen,
wobbly and swollen
with chemically-enhanced feed.

The industrial-sized stove here has eight
burners, all of them set on "HI," converging
into one awkward halo. This monumental flame
itself bursts into flame, but it's difficult to determine
if this new light is light, or another sort
of shadow, a source of heat, maybe peace, maybe
devastation, or what? The race car driver

thrashes hysterically for the invisible burning
that's all over his white jump suit
festooned with kaleidoscopic spark plug and laundry detergent ads.
His crew showers him down
with what looks like the artificial snow
you spray on your front window.
He goes limp. "Merry X-MAS!!!" Cut
to commercial. The Myth

of the Morning Star goes something like this: a little girl
on the Island of the Dead wants to aid her friends
in their long canoe journey to . . . I'm not sure where,
I wasn't listening too close then. The sun guides
by day, the moon and stars by night, so she will be

the Morning Star, transfigured into pure light,
fastened with a tether around her waist
so as not to sail out into forever.
But we know now that it's actually a planet: Venus.
And we know that the tether does get cut, and someone is lost
forever. An acquaintance of mine stopped me

on the street last night to tell me
of the conversation the two of us once had
which, frankly, I don't even remember,

but he says saved his life. I glance at the clock
on the building behind him as he talks.
I don't mean to do it, but he notices

and it breaks his heart. Respectfully
submitted. Darken the door. If love
really does raise the dead, please count me in.

T is for Total

This hydra lurks in the breast of each.
—Jean Cauvin

The files are packed fat with complaints, charges,
Death threats. Reports of death threats. During
An interminable car ride you somehow find out
About your brother's dire situation
And become all cold inside. There is also a curfew
Which is not to be toyed with—break it and hazard
Losing your bed for the night. From the blind

Side of a Chinese screen we listen to clients sweet-talk
The case workers, fire up mentholated cigarettes and spit
Smoke into their own laps. I guess I'm where
The buck stops, but I spend a lot of time shrugging
My shoulders, apologizing. It's not me, it's the system.
Granted, I did write the curriculum, but
What are you going to do? My hand was already like this

When I was born, resembling a tiny clump of premature
Raspberries. Seven operations later I have this: a fistful of grapes.
I've learned to accept it because it's the way I am. Kind
Of cute. This little slip of earth is broken, spoiled like the
black and red
Check sleeping bag in the attic that the possum cuddled
Into, died, and then evolved into a nation of maggots.
All cold inside. The retired battleship

Converted to a museum has come free from its
Moorings and floats aimlessly through the rainbow
Harbor butting into defunct piers and pleasure
Boaters. I'm stomping up and down on the bow,
Shrieking, trying to stop it, but how the hell could I ever
Stop it? Take a good look. What you thought
Was an ascot is really a tourniquet. What you hoped

Was an amiable little group of firemen huddled
In your backyard to preside over the downed
Electrical line twitching and sparking in the black grass
Is actually a fat, sweaty security guard stuffing you
Into one of those upright coffins from the Middle Ages
Lined with iron spikes. In you go. For awhile
You're able to forget about how bad it is;

The drenching fear recedes. Eventually,
Everyone is going to be beaten: some with many stripes,
Some with few. So we're all in this together, right?
Look at this welt on my back. Doesn't it look like an eggplant?
Misery loves more misery. Misery doesn't love. The road to hell
Isn't a road, it's a five-day convention in Albuquerque, New Mexico.
There's a place in Alaska where the sun saturates the valley

Nineteen hours a day, their produce is legendary: cannonball
Tomatoes, cannon zucchinis. The pot they grow is called
Matanuska Mindfuck, weed so potent you can't think
Of an adequate metaphor for it. At an emergency
Shelter in Detroit, a deaf photographer motions for a volunteer
To hold still while she ladles some withered
Green beans onto a homeless man's styrofoam plate

Vacation

On the first day of my summer vacation I stood in front of the drugstore. On the second day of my summer vacation I stood in front of the drugstore. On the third day of my summer vacation . . .

—Tony Nykodym

I'm wearing a love letter written in
invisible ink. I'm hot on the trail of the first
earwig of the day. Good morning to hope obscured!
to obscurity crouching quiet like a downed bird!
The days and nights arrive like pairs of children
holding hands, my wife stands in the center
of the room holding a vacuum like a cleaver,
she's got this look on her face:

We will prevail.

That's our feeling out here in the desolation,
and it feels good to have it—hope, I mean—
even if it is obscured. But only if it's not
dependent on how I flail around. God,
save me from my flailing. God, put an end
to the septic tank bones of deceit, put an end to
the bugs in our bed, and how catastrophes get played out
on TV, everything seen from above as from a helicopter
or a crossing guard's shoulder. Discard the orange belt
and be subject to all the vagaries of life, such as the prospect
of the guy who plays you in the made-for-TV movie
looking more like you than you do, cashing
your checks and cutting your grass with a smile
like a demonic eel on his face. So but when I said

"hope obscured," I wanted the operative word to be "hope."
Therefore I may start acting on the impulse I have

to approach strangers on the street and beg to be forgiven.
My mother caught the demonic eel in question. Only
I was raised in this town, as were my parents,
so there aren't many strangers to speak of, or to,
and everyone I know, I really do have to ask
forgiveness of those people. I *am* sorry

that you're paralyzed with dread at the thought
of disappearing, but I can't say I understand it.
Don't say the word "fear" 20,000 times per day.
See, I'm a lot more scared of getting bigger, more
of me to vie with, like an enormous cartoon
version of me, like how lots of food products
are sold by enormous cartoon versions of that same
food, e.g. the big pitcher of Kool-Aid, or that walking
double-cheeseburger at McDonalds. More of me
not praying. The elderly couple down the street
spend their days in lawn chairs in the garage watching the road.
My aunt tells me they've been at this for years.

But there must have been that first day.

So round, so firm, so fully packed
with bugs is the vacuum bag, mostly earwigs,
and we hope they're dead. Trace of campfires
wafting through the open car windows. I mean,
we *really* hope they're dead, because let's face it,
obscured is the only way we're going to get it.
I think when they cast the sitcom I'll ask
to play the dumb guy who's really sorta loveable.
Always getting into some wacky high jinks, but
he means well. And the problem is resolved
in about twenty-three minutes. Store-
bought fireworks gurgling up into the rural

sky. Lake water for the percolator. They stock
the lake with bass and bluegills, they call
the spray from the jet boats a rooster tail.

Recovering of Sight

I'm waiting for you through the tantrum wind
Drums its fifty fists against the window.

You're far from here. But don't I want to show

You what I do now? The luncheonette where
I get chocolate malts and my deaf neighbor

Nurses infant birds of prey to vigor.

A secret means of speech you and I devised,
Tapping on the plaster: one thump meaning

Yes, twenty-three for *Meet me in the hall.*

Even while I write this we're all moving,
Propelled and plunging like the days escape

Into regret here on the earth and in

The universe which will end, that has an end,
A center which wants to tell us our names.

Revolutions Per Minute

I go down every aisle
in the supermarket, I pretend
to read the list, my chest charged huge
and heavy in me by how
I could have it all, neatly
packaged, stacked, separated:
the chilled hum of spare ribs,
dish soap six lanes away,
the tea my wife asked for
right here in front of me.
The sky shifts, daylight grows
down through the grate in the ceiling,
touching the whole store at once,
marking my hand holding the list.
I take some and knead it
into the pitch of my heart,
smear it all over until
I'm gleaming black. I turn
to find sitcom characters mouthing the lines
I'm whispering to myself: *"If you don't get this*
cleaned up you're a dead man!" Yeah, I am—
like the condemned man in Kafka's *Penal Colony,*
his crime grooved into his skin
by the needle. I turn
again, I turn, I turn, I turn . . .

title: Triage

Definition of a disappointment, advanced upon warily
with lanterns and torches, weapons, apprehended,
yes, calibrated, collision tamed, repeat:
definition of a struck bell, lock picked, painted over
and solemnized, collared with unjustified hostility,
leaving pieces and jots of a branded
fraternity pledge shuddering beneath the volleyball
net. Wet. Also wrapped in cheesecloth, fondling each
other in the basement, on the dirt floor.
Also taught complex magnanimous routines, re-
named with the same name, straightened out with lye
and pronounced not dead on arrival,
just plain arrival. Transliterated. Taxidermied. Sold for
parts at discounted prices, then given away before the
closing bell to save face.
Lips. Noise. I said "sick." The driver kept replying, "Are
you soft?" Traditional conjecture arrived at by way of a
racing oval. *I was not offended.*
Many varieties of maniacs from which to choose—
which is a relief! Ladles, folding chairs and liturgical
furniture in storage in the drained pool,
yet retirees from the community keep surfacing with
goggles on their foreheads, towels yoking their necks.
Shown to the door
with much hostility. *Very often offended.* Rehearsals
held covertly in the gym, as well as harness racing
under investigation,
concurring with consumption of preposterous
amounts of alcohol, all of this set to a medley of
Romantic tunes in a recreational vehicle.
Warning: in all likelihood it will be 1:20 a.m. again
tonight, wherever you are. The fragrance of pencil lead
so intense it wakes the dog.
Big dog. What if the maniacs turned out to be right?
Good morning. Your toast, sir, smeared with what

looks, smells and tastes like creamed pencil lead
here in the Year of the Dragon, his (the dragon's) ornate grape yanking through the street, snapping after the shiny (luminous? radiant?) sphere.
But he does not. Get it. Still so very disappointed. Haydn's *Creation* rehearsed in the gymnasium, but performed in the sanctuary.
Monumental anticipation as the most severe dolor succumbs to sleep. Street sweeping as a career choice. Career. Career. Korea.

Range (Blastocyst?)

for Cyrus and Alisa

A full tank of gasoline. She implores us not
to leave, but we leave through the sky that is
both sky-high and in our faces with stone

snow descending wild,

proud, like an authority on bygone gangster
flicks who sticks his suet finger on my chest,
insists, "Jimmy Cagney never shit once,

I don't know about it." I know I no longer
light up a room. I know old friends are leaving
pensive messages on my machine, haltingly
suggest we get together soon. They imagine
me nursing a muffled drug habit, slumped
against the fridge, mouth ajar, eyes shining
and bored. Cheer up, kid, it's worse
than you think. The veil is lifted to reveal

another veil, but thicker; itchier too.
Your already lousy line of sight is eclipsed
by two guys holding up a banner demanding
more frequent garbage collection. Every day,
what was once of great use crammed in
a plastic bag and left at the curb, a golden
endowment for parasites. I'm still at a loss
to think that less than twenty-five years ago

Burt Reynolds was our country's leading film star.
To those of you reading this fifty years from now,
that may not seem like a big deal, but believe me,
it is. He's been replaced by Tom Cruise.

Maybe that too will seem absurd some day.
I used to mop the floors in a pre-school
at night, we'd replace the kids' folk song tapes

with Fugazi or The Replacements, the deafening gestalt
of meaningless anger marvelously incongruous
with the colorful plastic trucks and tiny tables.
The kids who attended that school then
have been replaced with other little kids,
they're pre-teens today, feeling how the word
"fuck" feels in their mouths. Forced into church
youth choirs. Trying on their older brother's
sport coat, way too big. Good luck, kid. Also,
FYI, the whole

identity crisis thing doesn't exactly get better
with time, so don't hold your breath. Instead,
how about just sit there for awhile

and wonder what it looks like

to be who you're supposed to be, bored
and pretending to read the *Institutes,* flipping
through the stations in a motel in the Midwest
that's getting pummeled by snow and reluctant
guests. It's Elvis' birthday, the King is
holding court on several channels at once
in many different guises: in prison garb,
in the round at his comeback concert, in
baby fat, then just plain fat, in the eyes
of a fawning teen with a scrapbook
clutched to her chest. She loves him because
he's beautiful. And I'm clutched by love, thus
on my way to being beautiful. And we
probably should have listened

to Alisa when she told us to stay, but though
she's beautiful, I was sure she only wanted us
to stay because she loves you. So we left against

her wishes and the counsel of the
radio voices. And the blizzard that absorbed us
is a famous one, so I won't mention her by name,
but rest assured it was a deeply nostalgic event
watching her work from the toasty confines
of the Dutch Pantry restaurant off I-80
in Pennsylvania. Even then I was at a loss,

woefully ill-equipped to clean up the radiant gore
marching out of me. Cleanse all the self-inflicted
wounds. Flies buzz near, on. Relinquish invisible
eggs. Hatch. Feed on bubbling abrasion. Repeat.
The chain of high command unbroken because I

insist
on leaping from zenith to nadir
at the serene insistence
of the devil.

OK, enough allegory. Did I mention the identity
crisis of the identity crisis? Did I mention
the odious sludge backing up nigh
the washing machine? Washing machine,
this is Vito. Vito, I'd like to introduce you to
the washing machine. Hello, you big white
metal box rocking like a terminal
egg. But it's not an egg anymore.

It's a chick, right?

Pissing my pants in the front seat
next to my dad on the way to Pennsylvania
was one of the more embarrassing events
of my life, but the funny thing is that
the joke he made about it (which involved
a tightly wound rubber band)
didn't make me feel worse, it made me
feel better. Go figure.

Against 5th Avenue

I feel good today, as if a breathless messenger
had just churned across town to deliver
the news to me: I've been elected
to write Floyd Patterson's autobiography
(and it was unanimous). I know it's silly
to be this rosy about the scaffolding
collapsing to the sidewalk, or the notion
of walking to the grocery store in a few minutes
to get some chocolate soy milk. When two
or three are gathered in a claw-foot tub
full of slugs, well, there you are, the three of you
standing in the slow-motion animals. Enjoy.
This definitely won't be the place I come
to fathom the mysteries of life, like the word
"shuttlecock," for instance, or why my wife woke me
up so early this morning—and just to watch her eat
Cream of Wheat! But I've got hold of this rudder,
need to get hold of this rudder to make the boat go fine,
watch me take my pulse with my fingers in a Scout sign.
Don't use the thumb, there's a mirror pulse in there.
The choir is well rehearsed, even if they're on fire,
even if my friends are forfeiting me to the volatile sons
of dentists, the fat slaughter of a pine tree. It smells
grand, but it feels not so good. Earlier we conduct
a mock interview on the front porch.

> Announcer: *So, do you think you're going to be able to*
> *turn it around in the second half? You're really getting*
> *whipped pretty good out there today; the Hawks are*
> *playing some great ball.*
> Maurice Cheeks: *Oh sure, Pat, I'm not worried, we're*
> *going to get Dr. J going in the second half, get some*
> *outside shots from Andrew Toney. And you'll see some*
> *outstanding 'D' from the Minister of Defense himself,*
> *Mr. Bobby Jones.*

Now we're looking for a front porch to sit on,

a bottle of beer planted between your feet and calling
out to passers-by, offering the stray dog
that's been hanging around to cordial-looking strangers.
I added the bit about slugs because we saw one
on the stairs last night in a video rental place. I was told
it was "the manager's problem," but now I'm telling you,
so you're to blame also, or to praise also, if the slug does
something nice, or if it holds out for a bigger contract.
He needs a home, he really does. There are messages
from distant stars on our machine. Salute the topless rebel
in my burnt-toast kitchen, then translate the slogan
and tell me what it means. I've been told, told, told,
but all I know is "corazon" means heart, the rest
I'm not sure of. Years ago, we never thought we'd be
in this bathroom drinking tequila with this future
anesthesiologist. One guy played the Cowardly Lion
in a community production, then donned face paint
and camouflage clothing and wandered into
the jungle, drunk, not to be seen again. If several
people call it "yes" then it must be "yes," yes? If
we all call it "no," then let's hope it's "no." I will call
this slug David. I will say this slug knows all
the Byzantine protocol of high stakes gambling.
I will get drunk and break a piece
of crystal and deny it and cry and scream like
a hungry baby on the floor, only to be soothed by
a dream of a photograph, a proposition,
a catch phrase, a semester-long thesis project
designed to divide pencils with erasers
from pencils *without* erasers. See it burning sluggishly
in the gravel parking lot? So much regret turned
to dark gray ash, and then you mourn for the ashes.
But I hate that I want to look back, salty tears

blasting out of my sockets, as if I knew all along
I'd want to weep again. But I'm going to be strong . . .
for the children.
Remove all the vowels and replace them with fleas. Find me
dozing in the park with a book about talking
rodents teetering on my knee, half-dreaming
of a firewall, going back and forth across the street
to get away from the sun and to get into the sun.

What Has Been Devoted to You

Steam and sunlight
like spiral stairs,
a panic cracks into mind:

the smell of a shower stall
burning so hot
that the fire goes out

and everyone leaves
the table
all at once.

Jesus comes to this
bleeding like a sema-
phore. He can see you through

the beveled glass. Smiling,
walking jilted, one foot
down in the gutter, one

on the curb. When
our ardent souls so unsound
leave mean tracks in the yard,

hands cupped 'round an ear.

Nothing in New York City

From a vast distance—the distance
traveled by a glass falling to the floor—
I will come to see you. I will advance
underground *("Stand clear the closing doors")*
into artificial light, I will sleep
right beside you all night. From another

town I'll come to be with you. Through the deep
brick-brown rivers, past jaundiced men covered
in garbage-bag plastic who run the halls
and bash out the lean bulbs with their fists, who
boot the car and guzzle gasoline. All
kinds of desperate laggards (muzzled, bored, blue
in the tooth) I've seen on my way up to your
room. My friend, four (truly five) flights up.

From the back of my thumb I'll come full-bore
to you, in Manhattan like an abrupt
caramel apple, a paintbrush through the core.
My black shoes tremble, becoming more
shined each block I put behind me, the door
to your place looming, and I can't ignore
that for you, my Heart, I am happy. Of
all the bodies in this billboard city,
yours is the one I look up to. Above
the street. The skyline. Airplanes. The stars. Me.

Neal Magee Birthday

Here's one dear ware I dare not ration, but I end
up being stingy anyhow, stuffing loose fragments
into the thick folds of my cape. And chocolate
smeared along the lips of all my pockets. That sound
you hear is a sorry, decrepit excuse hollered over
the dark racket of struggling bugs, but I'll more than understand

if you don't believe it. I don't believe it myself. I'm thinking of you
like a post on the corner in front of a church with a beard.
A regal, kindly tree with a beard. Citizen tree. The penalty
of the Big Town is the Big Stick, but on the subway down
to Wall Street, twitching and silver like a kinetic fish, the
dangling blade
seemed a little less threatening, a little chummy even. I tied on
my bib and we ate something in a marquee-lit deli. I can't remember
what. My advice to you: that swarm of foes around you
who roar like sirens will die out as quickly as burning thorns
if you've donned the correct hat—so choose carefully.
And if you want someone excited to see you, you've got it. Neal,

the bath I need is the one we all need, but I have to be forthright
and tell you, I've had on these same trousers for over a week now.
The undone stitch on the left cuff is red, not a blood red, but
an iron oxide red, sorta like damp earth, like clay.

For a Sick Friend

Autumn's majestic resignation
    Assembles in brown
        Clouds through the hall, insisting

That we learn to tremble
    For what is worth trembling
        For. That brick crack over

Your lip, a vertical line
    As this life is a vertical line,
        Begun at the hewn

Shoulder and finished at
    The fingertips. Five wet
        Pearls. The world sets

The rules and days against
    Which the body gets pressed,
        Then inevitably breaks through

With no warning at all, or endless,
    Awful warnings, the result is
        The same. Our frail frames,

So disposed to beauty, harbor death,
    Like the widow who carefully folds
        Her husband's clothes into boxes,

Then locks them in the cellar.
    The coupled socks. The underwear.
        But you bear about in your body

The dying of another, like the dust
    Manifests the light of the sun
        Descending on you in the hall,

A fiery copper down spout
    Delivering gifts from the perimeter
        Of heaven in a kicked gush.

Friday Night

Warm darkness spills over the trees, down
to the blood-green lawn, seeping into each
house in town through the shingles and the chimneys,
the splits in the river. He can hear it running
from his bright bathroom to where he's lying
in the yard staring up into the marriage
of sky, hope and dark.
He's drunk. He's thirty-one years old.
Crying and bleeding from certain
street signs, singing to himself about the day that lies
in wait behind his sore eyes,
trying to read something new
into his worn hands, the faded metal
fenders of his car parked in the road.
Streetlights are like counselors pouring sleep
into torn bottles all around him,
but the yard he rolls in is inside
another dream. Far away from birthdays
and garage sales and putting his kids to bed,
snapping the buttons on their pajamas
and kissing their wet heads. Out of sight from kissing.
This scares him so bad that he's afraid to move. He holds
his body hard as it lunges out of him. Tired and drunk,
he sleeps. He sleeps and dreams of baseball;
standing alone on the bases, unafraid, full. Easy to run,
to pull away from the hands that drag him back
into killing. Flying. Easing into the caramel jazz
of her weighty thighs. Wind. Waiting. Waking up
and walking back into his smiling life.
Waking up.

Automobile Accident

Who's fault is it but my own
for hiding once more in the Victrola?
The obvious is almost always
painful. My heaving breath while
Meggan fastened the handles with twine,
then the familiar shimmer of heat
rising from the chinking radiator,
then me in convulsion struggling to get free.

It's not until I've fought my way out
and the house empties
that the sobs are uncontrollable,
but even then it's not quite me. It's me
thinking of someone crying like that,
someone truly sorry for their sins,

rather than thrown from them
like a smoldering stick pulled from the fire
and pitched for a reckless dog.

There is no doubt that you too
will confront the constant scene:
car embracing fractured telephone
pole, styrofoam cooler of green
wine bottles exploded across
cul-de-sac, some stupid kid
suspended in the hedge beyond
the curb. Sticky blood between
his eyes. I'm telling you this
now so that you can think about
what you'll do before you get there,
how you'll manage when the supervisor
puts the manila folder in your hands.

Crying out of the corner of my eye

Afraid as I pad down to the bathroom with the night
in full swing, people scrolling past dead in my dreams
again, disgusted with me again. Inside the house
across the field a television stutters quiet and blue
like an artificial heart, a damp breeze lolling through
the screen, shut my eyes, listen through the edge
of the cat cries: I can't shake this. The moon, fallen
off its roost, exhales smoke in the dark, I remember
lying beside her in her loft, tapping her on the hip:
Do you know what that means? Jesus defeated

the ten leopards but when just one staggered back
to thank him only he was surprised. In the Delivery
Stall the cow tongues clean her calf, sticky with blood
plus all that other stuff inside of us, we're left with just
bliss, just adoption into God's own family, though
it doesn't feel like enough, which is why we were
crushed in the first place. Wade out into the wet
beans wracked with crickets and ask this question.
Climb into a tree to see it clearly. Through the dust

of the fair I saw you with a blonde child in your arms,
same hands, dropped my keys, arraigned on charges,
truck idling, I'm not asleep, I can't find my car, but I forgot
to tell you I hope you are fine and lie down at night
under a garment, under a wing. Cattle lowing, babies crying . . .
The bare bulbs strung through the animal barns like Christmas
lights, like bees whipping the heavy air as the sky collapses
from pink to dusk, I drive out past the whine of the Figure
8 race track, churning tall, brown clouds of dirt behind me.
I'm trying to create a quarantine in my head, but dear
old forgetfulness keeps plopping down her cute butt on
the davenport. Sometimes going to bed hungry is how things

work out. The same question. My wife whispers,
These spiders love you. We're both wet. It's time for us to sleep

together again until the night rises early again,
then we all rise in the electric light of the morning.

But the darkness in the morning is the darkness we can bear
because we know that what follows is sunlight.

The History of My Life

I was a weird little kid. But enough
About me. I remember
The morning the wind blew the sky
Anti-freeze green, driving our emergency
Rations off course so that our neighbors
Two towns over
Got the powdered milk, and we got
The tracts in Arabic
That read, "Proceed immediately
To your cellars,
Cover your ears and grimace."
Those were our lean years,
But it was fine by me. My happiness
Was looked after.
There was something exquisite just for me
In the squeaky Styrofoam
Cooler. Months passed. The afternoon
Began to arrive
Like a shift
Of new workers, clean shirts and packed
Lunch boxes. Only these guys were scabs,
And the union guys lobbed
Eggs and rocks
At their trucks. We were saved
From things getting too ugly
When the blizzard nobody can stand
Turned the corner
Asking who was up
For a few hands of Spades. We tried
To look busy,
But it was too late:
Some feeble membrane had been ruptured.
We looked
And felt regurgitated, then

Swallowed again. We wore
Flea collars. We chucked empty
Bottles of schnapps at little white
Girls
Playing jump rope. These were
Desperate times! My little brother
Was born premature,
Big as a regular-sized mouse,
Which made for
A very tiny brother. I kept him
Under the collar of my trenchcoat, trying to defend him
From the evil
Of this world. He ate ravenously and grew. He began
To bite people.
My mom finally gave me
The talk
About wild animals being happier
In the wild. *But Mom,*
he's my brother . . .
Do you think there's anyone left
Who remembers it the way I do?
People still come
To the poultry barn in the morning,
Speaking in humid
Circles. I thought we had survived.
But where are the frames and devices?
It's as if everything has dragged itself
Away, shrilling
Like a carousel as it went.
But I want to stay here.

Two

horse (hors) n. 1.a. A large hoofed animal *(Equus caballus)*, domesticated since ancient times and used for riding and for drawing or carrying loads. b. An adult male horse; a stallion.
2. A frame or device, usually with four legs, used for supporting or holding.
3. *Sports.* A piece of gymnastic equipment with an upholstered body used especially for vaulting.
4. *Slang.* Heroin.
5. Often horses. Horsepower.
6. Mounted soldiers; cavalry.
7. *Geology.* a. A block of rock interrupting a vein and containing no minerals. b. A large block of displaced rock that is caught along a fault.

—*American Heritage Dictionary*

I don't dis/integrate, *I go to work.*

—Robert Grenier

Arbeit macht frei (Work makes you free)

—slogan written on the gates of Auschwitz

Child with Bellows

The effortless chore, to make a killer of one's heart.

Eyes shaded by the blade of my hand
survey for some hero, some heroine

armed with a weapon for razing this crib . . .

It's spring again, they're mowing the thin
bands of grass between driveways and headstones

and you're still asleep, your face

turned in towards the couch, breathing in starts,
a bellows worked by a child

trying to keep the spent embers lit.

Temple, Temple

Smelling of cigarettes and construction
work, and your brief bow legs when you swagger
up the stairs to sing with us. You put your
lank, hard arms about me. You say, "You come
back to us." The heat is thick and wooden

against the worn windows which we prop
open, and our voices come out
like little breast pockets full of light. And Sister
sits with her arms on the sill, listening
from her room. O, the piano, like hands

above my heart. We rise up, arched
into the curve of the moon. We start
marching slowly around the room.

Horse Stories

for Scotty Utz

1.
The end of the night and the clock
alarm starts the familiar thump-cadence
of plumbing, bootsteps registering dimly
between rooms. I watch the lights appear
and fall dead on cue, keeping time on the daily
routine: the cereal spoon, the first cigarette.
Is it possible to see your face
in the mirror and not know it?
He tugs down the hooded sweatshirt, zips up the jacket;
can the back door be shut without waking us up?

It's not until the street that he pulls on
the headlights, cracks the window for another
smoke. He's driving to work down old farm roads,
ditches filled with orange-busted birds, the corn
rows cropped low, disclosing the soft brown bodies
of the does.

2.
The radio sent us to school through snow,
steamy, warm mornings in the portable,
blinking back the frosty sun on the rear
steps as we knocked out the erasers.

During Music, we filled the room with our
pinched voices; after Art, the walls pulsed
smeared, physical colors. We marched
single file to the big building for Gym,

to run the orange cones, climb the blue rope
to the ceiling, romp on the assorted
pieces of equipment that were shuffled
in and out. Off the gym was a utility room

where the janitor kept his brooms, black plastic
bags, a calendar with a faded photo-
graph of a woman in a bathing suit
sitting on a combine. He wore the same

clothes every day: green shirt rolled up, revealing
an uncertain tattoo above his thick
wrist; green pants with a clamorous key ring
on his hip; dull brown boots with copper eyes.

3.
Hitching my way to Anchorage
in the rain, the road nestled between
the muscles of the earth
on either side. This same rain
washed my dad's New Year's Eve
poker game out of our basement,
pouring taut and dull all day
long for four days, soaking
the legs of the sawhorses,
ruining our board games, staining
the carpet dark along the edges,
the streetlights droning like the grinding
machine in my father's shop. (He lost two
fingers in it when I was nine. I drew blood
on my hand with a pen, he wouldn't look
at me for weeks.) And the rain kept falling
in a stubborn rush, like the salmon
I'd seen running upstream, arching
their crisp scales in dumb strength
to get back to where the river
threw them out. Like the dead
salmon that eased down the belts
of the packing plant that whipped them

into shape for the Japanese buyer who knew
my name. I would dip the thermometer
down the fish's hole underneath, then
he would peer at me and ask *Yes?*
And I would reply *Yes,* even though
sometimes they were all warm as a mouth.
My foreman made me fudge the forms
before we turned them in.

4.
Weekends we sat on the living room floor
in front of the hulkish Zenith, watching
the lighter fighters, mostly Latinos
and Irish, and the heavyweights, all black
(save the occasional inflated white hope).
We drank tap water from a plastic gallon
milk jug, our bodies glistening in tandem
with the struggling fighters on the screen.
One Saturday, my father battled the wires
behind the set to pull in Ray Mancini's
lightweight title match with Duk-Koo Kim.
We were supposed to be on our way to a family
gathering, my mother fuming as the fighters
kept rising from their stools, my dad deadpan,
as he always was when watching boxing.
Finally, at the fourteenth round, Kim collapsed.
He entered a coma from which he never awoke,
ultimately dying from what Joyce Carol Oates
described as his "astonishing resilience and apparent
indefatigability. His 'heart' as it's known in boxing circles."

5.
He hadn't been there long when they told him
he'd won a turkey, "You can pick it up

in the cafeteria on the other side of the locker room."
When he came back empty-handed
they were laughing and smiling: F.N.G. Fucking New Guy.

There was Red, Teeta Burdette, Mess
(John Messamole). Heat Treat, a television
and radio in his cubbyhole, his magazines
and crossword puzzles. Harry Stump,
who was older, like a mentor to him.
And Jack, in charge of the precision tools.
Once you were his friend there was no need
to actually sign things out. (Buying him
a bottle of whiskey now and again wasn't
exactly a bad idea.) Someone stole

his Walkman before his family came
to pick up his tools and things. The whole
floor stopped when they arrived. His wife
was crying. None of them said a thing.

Repeat this phrase:
"What sort of hours are you willing to work?"

6.
After he leaves, she dreams the woods behind
the house, races with long legs
over rotting stumps and the stray
party garbage of nighttime teens, until
she slows down into a fall. She rolls over in the dark
maple mulch, resolved to pick herself up
and continue, but realizes that her feet
are bound up in hives and she's tired
enough to just stay down.

Like discreetly untying your apron
and dropping it as you head for the door.

The lake shaking itself free from the dog's coat
and hurrying back to the earth, eager not
to raise an eyebrow.

We keep driving an hour each way to work,
twelve hours, seven days, fiddling with the knob,
trying to pull the voice in just a little more clearly.

The bed is still warm where he left it,
and she's snoozing in synch with the radio.

7.
Having killed almost nothing in my life
(not any mammals, anyway; a snake once, thrown
off a bridge, and, of course, innumerable insects),
I stood rapt when a dried-out drunk I worked with
at a campground killed a groundhog with a .22
as it ambled along the edge of the little pond
behind the equipment shed. It slid into the water
with the report from the trees, dead. He resumed
his day like he had just snapped his fingers,
but I was dizzied, following him
into the barn where he hung
the gun back on the wall. We got into our electric
cart and floated off into the morning haze
buzzing alive with loud birds moaning
and alert squirrels hurrying out of sight.

8.
Work is where my father went.

9.
In 1987, Marvelous Marvin Hagler defended
his undisputed middleweight boxing crown
against "Sugar" Ray Leonard. Hagler lost in
a highly contentious decision, a bout where
he was the clear aggressor but where Leonard, the
showier, flashier fighter, poked the champ with thin
combinations—quick, glancing hits as Hagler pressed
onward like an elephant, head down and impervious
to Leonard's flicks. After the defeat,
Hagler never fought again. (He now works
as an action film star in Italy.)

My father was disgusted by the decision.
He was a great boxing fan, a great Hagler fan,
and he believed the judges had stolen Hagler's
belt from him. He loved Hagler for his fortitude,
his discipline in and out of the ring.
Leonard had thieved the title
with smoke and mirrors. He hadn't earned it.
"You have to take the champion's belt from him."

10.
I work there so you won't have to,
he told us from the front seat.
Do as I say, not as I do,

his inured dictum, and we knew it was true.
Food on the table, shoes on our feet:
I work hard so that you won't have to.

After a stabbed line drive he threw
his bat against the fence. He despised defeat.
Do as I say, not as I do,

he told me later, making sure I knew
that between wrong and right there lies a wide street.
I work here so you won't have to,

I'll cover the debts that accrue
to your score. Over and over our savior bleats:
Do as I say, not as I do,

reminding himself assiduously of who
he is; the mission he longed for:
I work hard so you won't have to.
Do as I say, not as I do.

11.
I'm always asking my cowboy friend Scotty (for whom
this poem is written) for the horror stories
about what he's killed and how. He showed me
the knife that slit a doe's throat after two passes
in the truck found it still stuck in the fencerow
("I made it easier on her and the coyote").
He laughed about the bobcat they shot
out of the only tree for miles, hiding it
in the freezer until its legal season.
Why did you kill a bobcat?
"They eat calves."
Bobcats have to eat too.
"Fine, let 'em eat someone else's calves."

12.
Donnie Marsh walked the railroad ties that hemmed
in the playground, talking to himself under
his hood, big-booted, lazy-eyed. His family
was poor, we ostracized him, the name "Marsh"
took on unsavory connotations *(Don't call me that)*.

Tony Tedesco strode there too, but with his head up.
Crazier, maybe, he'd tell us stories
about the Martians that talked to him,
or whatever we wanted, because we asked.
Cindy Curtain and Jenny Ford and a blonde girl
named Beth who wore cat glasses played Horses.
Lots of girls played Horses, alternating between
the splendorous animals that ran on their folders,
and the owners who cared for them. Other games
held the rest of us: jumprope; Smear the Queer;
tetherball; Red Rover; four square; guns.

13.
I never saw the inside of the factory
where my father worked. Pictured it like the image
in my social studies textbook of Henry Ford's first
assembly line: a grainy scene of thin men in
overalls and tweed caps attending to each side
of a Model A's chassis with a nebulous

tool. I saw the internally lit sign planted
at the entrance, flanked by the state and national
flags, the jammed parking lot (Don't Buy Jap Junk!),
the guard shack, the fast-food joints and 24-hour
liquor stores prowling the bounds of the property.

When driving by the plant, my dad would honk to his
friends, men I'd never seen but whose names he brought home
like the smell on his hands and breath: Doublemint gum, grease,
cigarettes and beer. Names I attend to now like
a zealous novice to a novena, naming
their names aloud again and again in order
to be blessed by them. Days, afternoons,

midnights, he left the house wearing
two plastic cards clipped below where his name
was written in script on his uniform: a small one
with a bar code for ID; and a larger, embossed one for hanging
outside of the stopped machines into which
he would crawl—a blurred head-shot
and bold red print which read:
"STOP!
Do not operate this machine!
My life is on the line!"

14.
Sonny Liston was his mother's twelfth child,
the youngest in a family of twenty-five.
Hardly schooled, he began working at age
eight in a sharecropper's field in Arkansas,
before following a chain of robberies and
assaults through several state pens to Mafia wages
and a title shot with Floyd

Patterson. Poor Patterson: a puffed-up
middleweight, he'd won the crown from another
slight heavy, Archie Moore, and he wore it
like a pitcher full of sour milk. A chagrined
ghost, he lost the title first to Ingemar Johansson
(who knocked him down seven times
in Yankee Stadium), and then for good
to the mighty Liston, who dismantled
him—Floyd frozen with dread—in the first
round of their first fight, repeating the feat
in the rematch. Both bouts were all
but over before the bell even rang: Patterson
brought a bag to both fights packed with food,

clothing, and a custom-made beard
and moustache for a covert getaway.

Liston lost his next fight to Cassius Clay,
and again to the new champ, now named
Ali, soon needing to revive the day
job he'd just left, as an enforcer for the Mob.
He settled in Las Vegas, where he drank
booze and shot craps and fished and broke
legs for small-time loansharks until his wife
found him six days dead in their home, his majestic
frame bloated, dried blood ringing his nose.
Most agree he was murdered—maybe by
a crooked cop, maybe by a friend incensed
that Liston wouldn't take a dive, by someone
who gave him a "hot shot": a lethal dose of heroin.
The autopsy revealed small portions of morphine
and codeine in his veins, evidence of the breakdown
of heroin, but the autopsy listed the cause of death
as lung congestion and heart failure.

The headstone at his grave reads:
"Charles 'Sonny' Liston, 1932-1970. A Man."

15.
You come back from work. There is silence, then
sleep, and still you do not want to talk. You
are not fully present. A part of you is always
catching up, arriving home
later, never really getting there. You
want very much to be idle, to want
nothing.

You sleep on the floor after work, jeans
or work pants, T-shirt, white cotton socks.
You sleep on your stomach, arms outstretched,
Sprawled, spread-eagle, like a boxer knocked
out, a hero fallen.

Three

Three Birds Arrive Tardy in Big Sur

July 25, 1972

Jayhawk
Jugular is what we're going for, no loss
Or swerve, nothing less than
His ghost to take up permanence in your chest. The
Nerve. Sundries. Peroxide used as mouthwash. He

Wrote the scroll, so let him read it.
I burned the cake, so let me have it.
Learned nothing about periscopes in submarine academy, so
Loaned myself out as a stuntman to the marshmallow factory.
Inquire. Pistol-whipped. Panoramic window. I'll say it
Again: pistol-whipped. Jiggle the handle, but what you're
Missing isn't worth missing and will take an

Entire life to evacuate,
Lies like "I have all my glasses" or "Will you
Last?" Stunned. Sliver of soap. Hidden
In the sofa, under the cushions, is death, which conceals
Life, your days numbered well. There are

3 members of the Trinity you needs be smitten w/.

Wren
Just when you thought the park was safe, they unearth another
Odd-shaped egg and determine it belongs to the
Huge backhoe that's been idle for almost
Nine years, rust about the edges like tribes of forsaken spider

Webs in the cellar, like a letter edged
In black is an announcement of death.
Larceny is another word for theft,
Like dolor is another word for despair. There
Is no word at all for birth unless you ask for it,

And then it will be given to you. Something is
Missing from the room you're in now: what is it?

Ecstasy is another word for rapture. The asthmatic cat
Laps milk out of a hubcap, trying to hoard all the
Love for himself. Haven't reckoned what's absent yet, have you?
I doubt you've even looked. Guess what?—The egg is a basketball
Spray-painted silver by some hooligans enacting a ludicrous hoax.

3 other words for hoax are: prank, ruse, and spoof.

Eagle
Jugular, that's what we're going for, then we'll shine unfurled to
Order out: sushi, ice cream & beer delivered on a bike by Thomas
Hearns. At the top of the invoice, a red stamp says "FINAL
NOTICE, Respond Today," so we memorize this earned certainty,

We decline out of the screen and into the spiny grips.
In a way, it's a comfort to have read ahead and know that
Long before the last chapter arrives we'll be
Losing so bad, most of the crowd will have ambled out of the arena,
Intent on listening to the rest of the slaughter in their cars.
As when they cut you off at the bar because you don't need one
More screwdriver. As when the scar on your neck drums
with a secluded, indignant pulse.

Endings are hard, especially when they're yours and they end it in
Lopping off the criminal's hand (especially hard when it's your hand).
Lots of people don't know it, but Jesus is coming again
In glory, and by glory I don't mean like a brass band. When he
Shouts, I'll dive on my face at his feet to sob "Help!" He'll wait

3 seconds, then we shall see his face;
and his name shall be in our foreheads.

Three Pictures of My Wife

I remember believing I could lose
You in New Orleans
Amidst
The bare-breasted coeds, jazz
Funerals, and family fortunes
Built on Tabasco sauce. Today
Fear still
Makes camp
On my gut, I've just got
Fresh culprits to blame.
There are about a thousand
Windows out
Our bathroom window, maybe
More, and I'm a little
Dazed
By the thought of all that
Potential tragedy. And
A man's shout
Up from the street
Covers the clock radio
In the bedroom.

* * *

The President is in town
Tonight, helicopters
Buzz the paralyzed
Traffic, near eye
Level with us
Here on the tenth floor.
My guess
Is that nothing can be seen

Through
The gauzy white curtains
Monique hung
Last month, but
I drop the blinds anyway
Before we put our bodies together.
"Our bodies together,"
That means sex, though
I don't know
What sex means.
Not "my orgasm"
Or "my desire,"
Not "my" anything.
If I wasn't

* * *

Here, that might be
Closer. Afterwards
We walk to the kitchen
To wrap the rhubarb pies
Cooling on the stove,
The Christmas lights strewn
Round the window
The only light
Until the refrigerator door
Soaks the brown tile floor in yellow. Now
I'll bet
We can be seen
If anyone cares to look:
She, kneeling there, naked,
Angling the last one
Behind the white wine.

Three Stories

for and after Lee

1. Keener Packing Co., Kenai, Alaska
To be on ice duty
means you have to be
there by four, which is the closest it comes
to night up here,
a low green dawn
whetted with the orange
that belongs to the sun alone,
just as the sun
is skipping off the horizon
like a hawk beating its wings in a frenzy
to halt its descent to the water,
then rising up with a fish in its hands
to take back to heaven. To enter
the icehouse you must climb
the zigzag staircase
bolted on the outside, duck
through the waist-high door that's like
the door on a sixties-era rocket,
then descend
the wide-runged ladder
on the inside.
All I remember
is the intoxication of work,
the hours poking
our long picks at
the auger to keep it running free, alternately
standing back from the solid gush,
just watching it work, then moving
to action, stabbing our tools stiffly
downward, violent even, as if to jab down
someone, the damned
moored-in ice gazing
up from the frozen ground in *Inferno* XXXII.

All I can remember is the auger
revolving indifferently
like a second hand,
deliberately chewing
the long flat slats of ice into handfuls
of ice, boxfuls of ice to keep the fish
on the dry dock cool
until we could process them. Stories
got passed from the foreman
as we worked: once a guy slipped
into the auger and got bit
clean to his knee. Another guy fell
and the auger grabbed hold
of the scruff of his sweatshirt
and held him tight to the floor, angled
just right over the small hole
so as to spare his life. I've also heard
that the Japanese buyers here
carry enormous amounts of cash
handcuffed to their wrists
in steel briefcases. I'm sure
you can finish that story yourself.

2. *Cipher*
Another story is the one about the Doberman
choking on the burglar's fingers. Another story
is a review I read in *The Ann Arbor News,* over
at the Faulkners', of Public Enemy's second album,
It Takes a Nation of Millions to Hold Us Back.
On the cover, Chuck D. and Flavor Flav are in
a prison cell, and the author attributes cataclysmic
significance to the fact that it's past eleven
on the clock hanging from Flav's neck. I heard

a horrifying story about a chubby middle-aged man
living in a town by himself who ran all over town
screaming about a man who lived in a house
by himself. Poised on a metal folding chair
in the middle of the kitchen with his mouth flapping,
moving up and down like a device for cutting,
sounds pouring out of his mouth like dead fish
out of a bucket. I mean a really big bucket,
more like a dumpster. It was completely out
of context. After a while a few people moved in
with him, so there's a context. It made a little more sense,
but not much. If you wake up after a power outage
and the clocks are all dead and there's no one home
you'll be without some of your context;
you might feel a little bewildered. Even if
there's no storm and everyone is home
it might be that way. They'll open their mouths
or show you some pieces of paper
with a lot of tiny black marks arranged neatly
in rows, but you'll have absolutely no clue
as to what it means. A beautiful woman might approach you
and put her arms around you and kiss you
on the mouth and you'll probably play along,
you'll kiss her back, even though you aren't sure
who she is or why she keeps asking you
to bring the basket up from downstairs. This place has a downstairs?
You're thinking to yourself, Maybe she'll want to sleep with me later.
You're thinking, Maybe she'll open up her blouse just for me.

3. *Death*
The coin can't find itself; it doesn't know
it's lost. It snuggles in the dust and keeps
a straight face.

The corpse doesn't know
that it's dead, but the dogs sure do,
perched at the door with their fur erect,
waiting for the nurses to let them out.

This isn't even me
talking right now and I'm a little bit scared
that I don't know who is. But what really scares me is the ghost
strolling at us across the lake. I'm scared he's going to say
my name. What scares me is that he won't.

The dogs are starting to moan, bloated
tears sliding down their snouts onto the black
linoleum, into a glove-shaped puddle, mimicking
the mouse blood brown and streaked on the baseboard.

Human blood isn't any bigger than mouse blood,
there's just more of it.

Imagine a swimming pool full of mouse blood.
Imagine dogs weeping. Imagine those dogs
resigning themselves to the inevitable, unlocking
their jaws and letting one coin each drop
from their melon tongues to the floor, then they themselves
dropping to the floor, dead.

Or
what they presume to be death since
they've never been dead before and don't know
what it feels like.

The dead aren't waiting
to be found. The dead aren't waiting for anything.

Jerry Quarry, Professional Record: 53-9-4, 33 KO's. Born May 15, 1945 in Los Angeles, California. Died January 3, 1999 in Templeton, California. A hard-hitting heavyweight contender who came along in a boxing era that many consider the best of all time, Quarry fought repeatedly for the championship yet never attained the title. *Boxing Illustrated* named Quarry the most popular professional boxer in the world in 1968 and 1969; in 1970 he shared the honor with Muhammad Ali. Quarry's most famous bout was against Ali in 1970, the first for Ali after a layoff of three-and-a-half years. Quarry lost, owing to the cuts that came so easily around his eyes. During a 1972 rematch, the fight was stopped after seven rounds, Quarry's face again covered in blood, a problem that was to dog him throughout his career . . . Some of Quarry's biggest victories came in the early 1970s (notably against Ron Lyle and Earnie Shavers), bouts which positioned him for a title fight against Joe Frazier. Quarry was knocked out by Frazier in a thrilling contest that saw both fighters staggered several times. Quarry never tried for the title again, though George Foreman has publicly stated that while he was champion, "I dodged him, purposely" . . . In 1975, Quarry announced his retirement, but as is so often the case with professional boxers, he was unable to resist the lure of the ring. He returned briefly in 1977, retired, then returned again in 1983—the same year that he was diagnosed with cerebral atrophy, brain damage caused by repeated blows to the head. His last comeback took place in 1992, when he participated in an unsanctioned fight in Colorado for the sum of $1050. He was soundly beaten in six rounds . . . In 1995 Quarry was inducted into the Boxing Hall of Fame, but by then he was suffering from dementia, his speech was noticeably slurred, and he could not even sign his name. He died of cardiac arrest while undergoing treatment for pneumonia.

—excerpted from *McClendon's Complete Encyclopedia of Professional Boxing*

photo by Monique Aiuto

Vito Aiuto was raised in Tecumseh, Michigan. He received a Master's degree from Princeton Theological Seminary, and has since worked as a pastor and as an outreach worker to the homeless. He is currently a Presbyterian minister in New York City. He lives in Brooklyn with his wife, Monique.

New Issues Poetry & Prose

Editor, Herbert Scott

Vito Aiuto, *Self-Portrait as Jerry Quarry*
James Armstrong, *Monument In A Summer Hat*
Michael Burkard, *Pennsylvania Collection Agency*
Anthony Butts, *Fifth Season*
Kevin Cantwell, *Something Black in the Green Part of Your Eye*
Gladys Cardiff, *A Bare Unpainted Table*
Kevin Clark, *In the Evening of No Warning*
Jim Daniels, *Night with Drive-By Shooting Stars*
Joseph Featherstone, *Brace's Cove*
Lisa Fishman, *The Deep Heart's Core Is a Suitcase*
Robert Grunst, *The Smallest Bird in North America*
Robert Haight, *Emergences and Spinner Falls*
Mark Halperin, *Time as Distance*
Myronn Hardy, *Approaching the Center*
Edward Haworth Hoeppner, *Rain Through High Windows*
Cynthia Hogue, *Flux*
Janet Kauffman, *Rot* (fiction)
Josie Kearns, *New Numbers*
Maurice Kilwein Guevara, *Autobiography of So-and-so: Poems in Prose*
Ruth Ellen Kocher, *When the Moon Knows You're Wandering*
Steve Langan, *Freezing*
Lance Larsen, *Erasable Walls*
David Dodd Lee, *Downsides of Fish Culture*
Deanne Lundin, *The Ginseng Hunter's Notebook*
Joy Manesiotis, *They Sing to Her Bones*
Sarah Mangold, *Household Mechanics*
David Marlatt, *A Hog Slaughtering Woman*
Gretchen Mattox, *Goodnight Architecture*
Paula McLain, *Less of Her*
Sarah Messer, *Bandit Letters*
Malena Mörling, *Ocean Avenue*
Julie Moulds, *The Woman with a Cubed Head*
Marsha de la O, *Black Hope*

C. Mikal Oness, *Water Becomes Bone*
Elizabeth Powell, *The Republic of Self*
Margaret Rabb, *Granite Dives*
Rebecca Reynolds, *Daughter of the Hangnail; The Bovine Two-Step*
Martha Rhodes, *Perfect Disappearance*
Beth Roberts, *Brief Moral History in Blue*
John Rybicki, *Traveling at High Speeds*
Mary Ann Samyn, *Inside the Yellow Dress*
Mark Scott, *Tactile Values*
Martha Serpas, *Côte Blanche*
Diane Seuss-Brakeman, *It Blows You Hollow*
Marc Sheehan, *Greatest Hits*
Sarah Jane Smith, *No Thanks—and Other Stories* (fiction)
Phillip Sterling, *Mutual Shores*
Angela Sorby, *Distance Learning*
Russell Thorburn, *Approximate Desire*
Rodney Torreson, *A Breathable Light*
Robert VanderMolen, *Breath*
Martin Walls, *Small Human Detail in Care of National Trust*
Patricia Jabbeh Wesley, *Before the Palm Could Bloom: Poems of Africa*